<< *Native Americans in History* >>

NATIVE AMERICANS
in History

A HISTORY BOOK FOR KIDS

Jimmy Beason

Illustrations by Amanda Lenz

ROCKRIDGE
PRESS

Series Designer: William Mack
Interior and Cover Designer: John Clifford
Art Producer: Sue Bischofberger
Editor: Mary Colgan
Production Editor: Andrew Yackira
Production Manager: Michael Kay

Illustrations © 2021 Amanda Lenz
Author photo courtesy of Ramona Cliff
Illustrator photo courtesy of Mai Anh Nguyen

ISBN: Print 978-1-64876-288-8 | eBook 978-1-64876-289-5
R0

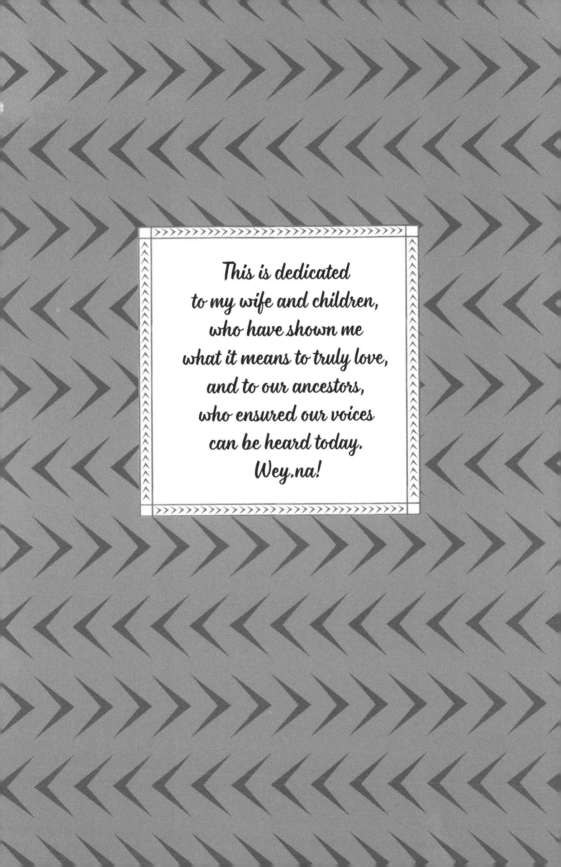

This is dedicated
to my wife and children,
who have shown me
what it means to truly love,
and to our ancestors,
who ensured our voices
can be heard today.
Wey.na!

Contents

Introduction viii

SEQUOYAH 1

TECUMSEH 7

SITTING BULL 13

GERONIMO 19

ZITKALA-SA 25

Jim THORPE 31

Maria TALLCHIEF 37

Susan LaFLESCHE 43

Bertha PARKER CODY 49

Vine DELORIA JR. 55

Russell CHARLES MEANS 61

Wilma PEARL MANKILLER 67

Suzan SHOWN HARJO 73

John BENNETT HERRINGTON 79

Debra ANNE HAALAND 85

Glossary 91

Resources 97

References 99

Introduction

Ha.we! It is an honor to share with readers an overview of historical and contemporary **indigenous** people. There are many important Native American people who have captured the attention of scholars and readers over the years. The individuals you are going to read about are only a few out of many. They were chosen to represent the diversity of experiences among different native people. Some are renowned for protecting their homelands and communities during the early phases of American **colonization**. More recent native figures are known for their enduring spirit in the face of many obstacles.

At one time, native people were reportedly a "vanishing race." This unfortunate perspective led many Americans to believe that native people had disappeared. What you read here should dispel this myth. Native people are still here and have continued to move forward. Regardless of background and tribal nation, native people are thriving with the strength of their **ancestors**.

Sitting Bull led with **spiritual** guidance and a determined will. Maria Tallchief stayed true to her Osage **heritage** as she broke barriers in ballet. Tecumseh was a gifted speaker who inspired many **warriors** to protect their communities from American hostility. Jim Thorpe was a quiet man who led by example with his superb athletic abilities and showed the world that a native man could win Olympic gold.

One thing they all have in common is how they learned to survive in a world that was outwardly **hostile** to them for simply being natives. Beginning in 1492, European colonization brought dire consequences to indigenous people. After the Americans won their independence in 1776, native people began to lose theirs. They were forced from their territories and homelands. They were not allowed to hunt and plant crops as their ancestors had done. Their spirituality was outlawed. Not until 1978 were native people legally allowed to practice their religion again. Today, indigenous people are continuing to recover from these historical **injustices**.

And yet, they have continued to resist forced assimilation and have stayed true to their values. Despite turmoil, an underlying feeling of unwavering hope prevailed. Hope for a better life. Hope for a better future. Hope that what they were doing would solidify the strength of future generations. Native values always kept the children in mind, with a goal of positively impacting the grandchildren still to come.

As you read these stories, think about your own life. Think about the contributions you will make toward your family and community, and how your determination to do great things can inspire others to do the same. We all have talents, skills, and abilities. Know that you can use these to create a better world for others. Sometimes, we think we are not able to create changes. But the stories here demonstrate that individual achievements today can make a lasting impact on and provide lessons for future generations. So, be inspired and move forward with a strong will and determination that you can make your life the best it can be.

SEQUOYAH

{ circa 1760–1843 }

CHEROKEE

Sequoyah is best known for developing the first Native American writing system in North America. His writing system helped preserve the history, language, and **culture** of the Cherokee people. The Cherokee **syllabary** is still used by the Cherokee people to this day.

Sequoyah may have been born between 1760 and 1776 in Tuskegee, a Cherokee settlement in eastern Tennessee. *Sequoyah* translates into English as "pig's foot." This name may have been a reference to a problem with his foot he either was born with or got later from an injury. His mom belonged to the Red Paint Clan. Her name was Wu-te-he. The Cherokee have seven clans. Clans are smaller groups of families and kinfolk within the larger tribe. His father may have gone by the name Nathaniel Gist. When Sequoyah grew up, he used the English name George Gist. Sometimes, he wrote down his last name as "Guess" or "Guest." Historians believe his dad could have been a soldier, diplomat, or merchant.

Sequoyah belonged to an important Cherokee family. Wu-te-he had five brothers who were respected leaders. Sequoyah's uncles were known for opposing white colonialism. Sequoyah also had two brothers, Dutch and Tobacco Will, who were important figures in Cherokee society. Dutch was a respected leader, and Tobacco Will supported and signed the Cherokee Constitution, a document designed to counter white stereotypes of natives as savages, resist white **encroachment** into their lands, and cement the tribe's **sovereignty**.

As a child, Sequoyah would have been strapped into a cradleboard and placed in a tree to sleep. Cradleboards were thin boards with leather or cloth straps. They kept babies warm and secure. During his waking hours, he would have watched his mother work in the crop fields.

Sequoyah would have helped his mom work in the fields when he got older. The Cherokee were farmers and lived in settlements. They harvested beans, pumpkins, and squash. When Europeans arrived, they brought watermelon and peaches. The Cherokee started growing these, too. Europeans also brought horses, which the Cherokee started using for farm work.

Sequoyah was a creative boy. He crushed together berries and leaves to make paintings of people and animals. He also carved animal figures out of wood. Sequoyah was fond of making small stick houses out in the forest as well. When he was around 15, he would have started defense training, using **tomahawks**, spears, and bows. Cherokee boys learned about having patience and withstanding hunger by sitting out in the woods for hours.

He would have learned how to hunt around this time. The Cherokee word for hunting is *ga-no-ha-li-do*. Sequoyah would have learned how to hunt rabbits and squirrels using a blowgun, a wooden tube used to shoot darts with your breath. Cherokee men hunted deer, turkey, and other animals. They would eat the meat and make tools out of the bones. Cherokee hunters said prayers for the lives of the animals they killed. This was out of respect for what the animals provided to help the people live.

When Sequoyah got older, he would have joined the men. They made bows from hickory trees and arrows from a type of bamboo called rivercane. Arrowheads were made from **flint**. When Europeans arrived, the Cherokee traded the animals they hunted for European tools.

Sequoyah would have learned about conflict by playing stickball. In this game, Cherokees used sticks with small, round nets at one end to pick up a small ball. The players then had to run with the ball and throw it into the other team's scoring area. The other team could bump into the ball carrier and make physical contact. Lacrosse is based on the game of stickball.

As an adult, Sequoyah had a limp. He may have had polio as a child or been wounded in a hunting accident. Historians are not sure. He became more involved in trade. His mother also worked as a trader, and when she passed away, he started a silversmithing business. Silversmiths molded bits of silver into utensils, jewelry, and other decorations. Through his trading business, he discovered the importance of writing.

Cherokee people had an **oral tradition**. That meant that stories were passed down through word of mouth only. Some of Sequoyah's friends thought writing was a form of witchcraft. He did not believe them and started creating Cherokee syllables.

Sequoyah was not able to complete his writing system during this time because he joined the US Army to fight in the War of 1812. He fought alongside Andrew Jackson, who later became president, at the Battle of Tallushatchee and the Battle of Horseshoe Bend. His time spent with soldiers allowed him to study writing close up.

Sequoyah wanted the Cherokee to have their own language writing system so that they could be more independent from white Americans. He spent a decade coming up with the system. He created 85 syllables to represent the Cherokee language. Any Cherokee who knew the language and learned the symbols could read and write in Cherokee. By 1826, thousands of Cherokee people were far more **literate** than their white neighbors. Sequoyah's syllabary was used to print almanacs, government documents, and Bibles.

A **missionary** named Samuel Worcester helped make Sequoyah's writing system popular. He thought the Cherokee writing system would help "spread the gospel."

> **"IF OUR PEOPLE THINK I AM MAKING A FOOL OF MYSELF, YOU MAY TELL THEM THAT WHAT I AM DOING WILL NOT MAKE FOOLS OF THEM. THEY DID NOT CAUSE ME TO BEGIN, AND THEY SHALL NOT CAUSE ME TO STOP."**

By 1828, the Cherokee had published the first-ever Native American newspaper. The Cherokee paper was called the *Cherokee Phoenix*. Articles were printed in both Cherokee and English.

Sequoyah's writing system created a sense of pride and preserved important Cherokee events, history, and traditions. Sequoyah died in 1843. By this time, more than four million pages of books, Bibles, and news articles had been printed in his Cherokee system. Sequoyah's writing system took years to perfect, and his contributions will benefit Cherokees for years to come.

THINK IT THROUGH
Why are reading and writing important? Think of as many reasons as you can.

EXPLORE MORE!
Learn more about the Cherokee Nation, its government, and its culture, and even learn its language, at the Cherokee Nation website, Cherokee.org.

TECUMSEH

{ circa 1768–1813 }

SHAWNEE

Tecumseh was a war leader of the Crouching Panther Clan of the Shawnee tribe. He was a great speaker. Tecumseh told different native communities to see themselves as *one* people, a single culture. He is best known for building a **confederacy** of native warriors to protect their lands from the white Americans' invasion.

Historians believe Tecumseh was born around 1768 at the Shawnee village of Piqua near the Scioto River of present-day Ohio. *Shawnee* means "southerners" in the Algonquin language spoken by the tribe. Tecumseh's name roughly translates into "shooting star." Tecumseh's mother, Methoataske, who was from the Muscogee Creek, had eight children with his father, Puckeshinwa.

Tecumseh's young life started on a tragic note. The Virginia governor, Lord Dunmore, sent 1,100 Kentucky **militiamen** toward Shawnee villages. They were seeking revenge for the killing of **settlers** in eastern Ohio. Shawnee leader Cornstalk summoned 300 warriors to attack the militiamen before they reached the villages. The Shawnee offered strong resistance but were forced to retreat. Tecumseh's father was killed during this battle, known as Lord Dunmore's War. Tecumseh was six.

After her husband was killed, Tecumseh's mother either returned to her Muscogee Creek relatives or traveled west in 1779 with other Shawnees. Either way, the children lost both of their parents. Shawnee Chief Blackfish became a father figure to them. Tecumseh's older brother, Cheeseekau, taught him the ways of Shawnee warriors. His older sister, Tecumpease, taught him Shawnee cultural values.

Around the age of 15, Tecumseh began to join his brother on raids against white American settlers. When Tecumseh was 20 years old, he wounded his thighbone while on a raid and developed a limp. A few years later, Cheeseekau was killed in a battle in Tennessee. Despite these challenges, Tecumseh married twice and fathered a son. During this time, he began to see the need for native people to unite to protect their lands.

After Great Britain lost the Revolutionary War, the country signed the **Treaty** of Paris in 1783. This treaty "gave" the Americans the land claimed by the British. However, native leaders did not sign this treaty. When more Americans started moving into native territory, Miami leader Little Turtle organized the Northwest Indian Confederacy to keep them out. Tecumseh served as a **scout** for the confederacy.

This battle was the confederacy's biggest victory. They defeated almost 1,000 US troops. However, the confederacy lost the Battle of Fallen Timbers in 1794 and signed a treaty that gave the Americans more land. Tecumseh was upset with the outcome and moved to Indiana territory.

There, Tecumseh's village came under threat. William Henry Harrison was the governor of the Indiana territory. He persuaded leaders from the Wyandotte, Kaskaskia, and Kickapoo tribes to give away more land in the territory. Tecumseh felt they had no choice but to keep fighting. He wanted to create a new alliance that was bigger than Little Turtle's confederacy. His younger brother Lalawitheka felt the same way.

Lalawitheka struggled with alcoholism. One day, he was very drunk and fell into a firepit. His family thought he was dead and prepared him for a funeral. Instead, he woke up and told his family about a vision he had seen. He said the Great Spirit told him the Shawnee and other natives needed to reject European food, clothing, housing, and tools. He quit drinking alcohol and became a spiritual mentor with a new name—Tenskwatawa, or "the open door."

Tecumseh's speaking skills and his brother's spiritual teachings helped **recruit** more warriors to his alliance. Tecumseh persuaded the Potawatomie, Miami, Shawnee, Delaware, Ojibwe, Kickapoo, and Ottawa to join. All of his followers moved together to a new village across the Ohio border in white American territory. They called their village Prophetstown.

Tecumseh met with Governor Harrison to oppose more land being taken. Harrison viewed Tecumseh's new confederacy as a barrier to getting more lands and wanted to get rid of them. In 1811, Harrison led 970 militiamen to Prophetstown. Tenskwatawa sent warriors to attack Harrison's camp. Around 200 soldiers were killed. Many native warriors were killed, too, although there was no exact count. Harrison regrouped and marched directly into Prophetstown. The village was abandoned, so he declared "victory."

Harrison thought Tecumseh's confederacy was over. But after Tecumseh returned, he asked the British for more weapons and resources to continue warring with the white Americans. He got his chance when the War of 1812 started. His warriors defeated white Americans in battle at Fort Meigs. They killed 600 US soldiers and militiamen at the Battle of River Raisin. They chased off and threatened US settlers living in the area as well.

Despite Tecumseh's victories, the British military was not as successful. They lost the battle for the Great Lakes and had to run away from Harrison's forces. British General Henry Procter tried to make a last stand against the US military near the Thames River. Tecumseh and 500 of his allies showed up and provided support.

However, Colonel Richard Mentor Johnson charged through the native and British lines. The British retreated, but Tecumseh and his warriors stayed and fought the white Americans in the swamps. Tecumseh

> **"I AM A SHAWNEE. MY FOREFATHERS WERE WARRIORS. THEIR SON IS A WARRIOR. FROM THEM I TAKE MY ONLY EXISTENCE. FROM MY TRIBE I TAKE NOTHING. I HAVE MADE MYSELF WHAT I AM."**

was shot and killed. Word spread about his death and the warriors agreed to stop fighting. It was October 5, 1813.

Mystery surrounded Tecumseh's death. One story suggested he was buried in a secret location. Colonel Johnson said he shot and killed Tecumseh. In any case, US soldiers mutilated the body believed to be Tecumseh's.

Tecumseh was admired by both his allies and his enemies. His life serves as an example for all to continue fighting for what you believe in.

THINK IT THROUGH

Why do you think Tecumseh and his warriors helped the British soldiers when they were in trouble?

EXPLORE MORE!

Learn about the Shawnee Tribe, read a message from the chief, and do a deep dive into the tribe's history at Shawnee-Tribe.org.

SITTING BULL
{ circa 1831–1890 }
HUNKPAPA LAKOTA

Sitting Bull was a warrior, **medicine man**, and spiritual leader of the Lakota. His leadership guided warriors at the Battle of Little Bighorn. He also expanded Lakota hunting territory and **advocated** for his people.

Sitting Bull was born around 1831 near Grand River in present-day South Dakota. He was part of the Oceti Sakowin, or "seven council fires." The Oceti Sakowin refer to the Lakota, Dakota, and Nakota tribes of the Great Plains. These tribes had different lifestyles and language **dialects**. Lakota, Dakota, and Nakota mean "allies." Each tribe also had different subdivisions, or bands. Sitting Bull was from the Hunkpapa band of the Lakota. *Hunkpapa* means "head of the circle" or "at the entrance."

Sitting Bull's first name was Jumping Badger. He earned the name Sitting Bull during a battle with the Crow tribe when he was 14. He counted coup on a Crow warrior. "Counting coup" means hitting an enemy with your hand or a "coup stick" without killing them or getting killed. Because of this brave deed, he earned his father's name, Sitting Bull. He also joined the warriors circle.

Sitting Bull married his first wife when he was about 20 years old. Unfortunately, she died giving birth. Several years later, his father also passed away. Sitting Bull married twice more and fathered two daughters and a son. He also adopted his nephew, One Bull.

Sitting Bull fought his first battle with US soldiers in June 1863 as a part of the Dakota War. The Hunkpapa were not directly involved with the Dakota War. However, the US Army attacked them, mistaking them for their Dakota relatives. Lakota and US hostilities increased when white American **buffalo** hunters killed thousands of buffalo and left them to rot. The Lakota relied on the buffalo for their food, clothing, and shelter.

In 1868, the Lakota signed the Fort Laramie Treaty with the United States. It promised the southwest portion of South Dakota as the Lakota **reservation**. By this time, Sitting Bull was leader of the Hunkpapa. He was upset the treaty was broken not long after it was made. Gold was discovered in the **Black Hills**, and President Ulysses Grant's administration said gold miners needed full access to the area. The Black Hills were on Lakota territory and were held **sacred**.

US officials from Washington, D.C., attempted to buy the Black Hills from the Lakota, but they refused to sell.

However, the United States figured simply offering the money was enough to claim ownership of the Black Hills. Sitting Bull and his camp were hunting north of that area, near the Powder River in Montana territory, as **game** was becoming scarcer in the southern plains.

The Lakota who were away from their reservation were ordered to return and report to the reservation agency, which was in southern South Dakota. Reservation agencies were small outposts where US officials provided **rations** and other goods as part of treaty agreements.

The order was made in December 1875. The Lakota were supposed to be back on their reservations by January 31, 1876. It was nearly impossible for Sitting Bull's people to move back by the government's deadline. They were 240 miles away and the winter weather was severe.

On February 7, 1876, the United States authorized military operations against Sitting Bull and his people. General Philip Sheridan ordered General George Crook to march into the Lakota stronghold in Montana territory. Sitting Bull inspired the Lakota, Cheyenne, and Arapaho to help protect their camp. Altogether, there were 5,000 warriors. This led to the Battle of the Rosebud. Sitting Bull's warriors defeated 1,500 soldiers.

Sitting Bull decided to move to the Little Bighorn River after their victory. They held a Sun Dance ceremony while they were camped, and Sitting Bull danced and fasted for three days straight. He said he had a spiritual vision in which US soldiers fell headfirst into their camp like "grasshoppers." He said the creator was offering these soldiers up to be killed because they would not listen.

On June 25, General George Armstrong Custer attacked the Lakota camp. General Custer was known as an "Indian fighter." Custer was killed, along with the entire seventh **cavalry**. This became known as the Battle of the Little Bighorn. General Sheridan added another 2,500 soldiers to move against the Lakota. Meanwhile, the Black Hills were taken in direct violation of the 1868 Fort Laramie Treaty.

Sitting Bull refused to give in and moved a couple hundred miles north into Canada with his followers. However, life became more difficult. Buffalo were becoming scarce, and Sitting Bull's group was beginning to starve. On July 19, 1881, he finally surrendered to US officials.

He eventually lived on the Standing Rock Reservation after spending two years in Fort Randall as a prisoner. Then he traveled as a performer in Buffalo Bill's Wild West Show. Buffalo Bill Cody was a former military scout turned showman. His shows were reenactments of battles from the "Indian Wars." Sitting Bull rode on a horse for the white audience.

In his final days, Sitting Bull lived in a cabin on the Standing Rock Reservation with his children and two wives. Although he shunned Christianity, he sent his children to Christian schools so they could learn to read and write.

> **"LET US PUT OUR MINDS TOGETHER AND SEE WHAT LIFE WE CAN MAKE FOR OUR CHILDREN."**

In 1890, Sitting Bull was convinced to take up the Ghost Dance started by Wovoka, a Pauite man. He said the dance would bring back the old ways. However, white officials viewed dancing as preparation for war. On December 15, 1890, the Indian police were sent to arrest Sitting Bull. The Indian police were other Lakota who worked for the US government. Sitting Bull's followers and the Indian police shot at each other. His son, Crow Foot, was shot dead. Then Sitting Bull was shot twice and killed, too. He was 58 years old.

The life of Sitting Bull is one of honor, dignity, and loyalty to the Lakota way of life. He set an example of bravery and commitment to Lakota culture and values. Because of this, his spirit lives on.

THINK IT THROUGH

What are some qualities of a good leader? How did Sitting Bull show those qualities?

EXPLORE MORE!

Learn about the government, culture, and history of the Rosebud Sioux Tribe of South Dakota at RosebudSiouxTribe-NSN.gov.

GERONIMO

{ *circa 1825–1909* }

APACHE

Geronimo was an Apache warrior and medicine man who led fellow Apaches in battle against US and Mexican troops. He was never captured by either side. He is known today for his courage, fierceness in battle, and desire to remain free.

Geronimo was born around 1825 on the Arizona–New Mexico border, near Gila River. Mexican soldiers reportedly gave him the name "Geronimo," which is Spanish for St. Jerome, a Catholic saint of lost causes. His Apache name was Goyathlay, meaning "One Who Yawns."

In his autobiography, Geronimo recalled playing on the dirt floor of his father's lodge. As a baby, his mother kept him close while she tended the crops—melons, corn, and beans. When he became a young man, he learned how to run fast for long distances. He also started hunting turkeys, deer, buffalo, and rabbits. He hunted bears and mountain lions with a spear. Their fur and skins provided shelter and blankets.

19

In 1846, he joined the warriors council. Young Apache men could become warriors after they came along on four war parties. Geronimo cared for the horses of older warriors. He also had to cook and do chores without being told. During his warrior training, he followed the Apache leader, Mangas Colorado, on raids into Mexico.

After proving himself as a warrior, Geronimo married an Apache woman, Alope, and they had three children together. Geronimo gave Alope's dad horses to secure their marriage, which was part of their tradition. He built a lodge near his mother's place. It was made of buffalo hides and mountain lion skins. His wife decorated their home with artwork from beads and drawings on **buckskins**. Geronimo and his wife taught their children the same Apache traditions they had learned.

Although the Apache were one group, there were various kinship groups within the Apache living in different locations. Geronimo was from the Bedonkohe band of Apache. However, he considered himself Chiricahua as well after he joined Cochise's band. Cochise was a famous Apache resistance leader. Geronimo picked up a lot of the anger he later felt toward the white Americans from his friendship with Cochise.

At first, relations between the Apache and the white Americans were friendly, and they traded goods peacefully. That changed when a local rancher accused Cochise's band of stealing cattle and kidnapping a young boy. Cochise denied the charges and escaped when the US Army tried to arrest him. This led to Cochise killing three white soldiers and the Army hanging three of his nephews. The Apaches now considered the white Americans enemies.

In 1858, Geronimo and other Apaches went to Janos, Mexico, to trade. While they were away, 400 Mexican soldiers attacked their unguarded village. Around 100 Apache women and children were killed. Among the dead were Geronimo's mother, his wife, and their three children.

Geronimo pursued a path of war and vengeance that lasted 28 years. He led raids into Mexico and attacked US settlements. In 1882, Geronimo and his followers killed Juan Mata Ortiz as revenge for the attack on their village. He was the local commander of the Mexican Army.

Geronimo and his Apache **guerrilla fighters** could travel 15 hours per day and cover 40–60 miles on foot. Their favorite method of battling US and Mexican soldiers was setting up an ambush, or surprise attack. When the attack was over, they took supplies from the dead soldiers and moved to another location.

There was no official declaration of war between the Apache and white Americans. Conflict gradually began after gold miners, merchants, scalp hunters, and settlers intruded into Apache lands. These groups would start trouble with the Apaches, then demand that the US Army protect them.

After Cochise died from an unknown illness in 1874, Geronimo kept fighting the United States with Naiche, Cochise's son. Geronimo's reputation as a skilled warrior continued to grow. In 1878, Geronimo helped rescue the Apache leader "Loco" and several hundred of his followers from the San Carlos Reservation, where 3,000 US troops were patrolling. The US Army wasn't able to stop Geronimo's group. The number of troops increased to 5,000, even though they were tasked with finding only 35 Apaches.

In March 1886, Geronimo appeared to give up, but changed his mind shortly before he was to turn himself in. For several months, Geronimo and his band continued to go on raids all over the southwest. Then, in September 1886, he sent word that he was ready to surrender. General Nelson Miles, who replaced General Crook, met with Geronimo in Skeleton Canyon, Arizona. This time, Geronimo, along with many of his followers, laid down their rifles.

Geronimo and his band of Apache resistance fighters boarded a train as **prisoners of war**. They were being sent to Fort Marion, Florida. Apache scouts who helped the US Army locate Geronimo were also imprisoned. There they were sentenced to hard labor. They dug trenches and **latrines** and rebuilt parts of the fort. Conditions were not good. Hundreds of Apache prisoners died from disease at Fort Marion. They were eventually transferred to Mount Vernon, Alabama, where Geronimo became a justice of the peace. He was paid $10 a week to maintain order.

At the time of his capture, Geronimo was a living legend. White folks bought mementos and autographed pictures of Geronimo at county fairs. When Theodore

> **"WE ARE ALL CHILDREN OF THE ONE GOD. GOD IS LISTENING TO ME. THE SUN, THE DARKNESS, THE WINDS, ARE ALL LISTENING TO WHAT WE NOW SAY."**

Roosevelt became president of the United States in 1905, Geronimo marched in the inaugural parade. Even though he traveled, he was still a prisoner of war and would spend his last days at Fort Sill, Oklahoma. Local white citizens kept him from returning to Arizona.

Then, in February 1909, Geronimo passed away from pneumonia. He was 80 years old. Geronimo was buried in the Apache Prisoner of War Cemetery in Fort Sill. His life and **legacy** still serve as an inspiration to many within the native community.

THINK IT THROUGH

How do you think Geronimo felt about going to county fairs and signing autographs? How would you feel?

EXPLORE MORE!

Learn about the Chiricahua Apache Nation, including their history, culture, and values, at ChiricahuaApacheNation.org.

ZITKALA-SA

{ 1876–1938 }

YANKTON DAKOTA

Zitkala-Sa was born in February 1876 on the Yankton Indian Reservation in South Dakota. Her mother was Dakota and her father was a white man. Zitkala-Sa means "Red Bird" in English. She also went by the name Gertrude Simmons Bonnin. Zitkala-Sa was only eight when Christian missionaries visited her reservation to recruit native children for a boarding school in Indiana.

Her mother did not want to send her away. To persuade native children to go to the school, the missionaries told children they could ride on trains and visit huge apple orchards. The Indian boarding schools were places where children were told they could not be "Indians" anymore. They were forced to speak English and go to a Christian church. Some were forced to go by the government. Many children were abused. Unfortunately, many native parents did not know about their children being hurt until they came home.

Zitkala-Sa's mother eventually let her go. Dakota culture seemed to be ending, and she wanted her kids to have a "white man's education." Also, Zitkala-Sa wanted to go after hearing the missionaries' wonderful stories. But when Zitkala-Sa arrived at the school, she was extremely upset. All the children had to get haircuts. Her mother had told her how their enemies would cut the hair of cowardly Dakota warriors caught in battle. Dakota people only cut their hair in **mourning** when a loved one died. The school staff tied her down to a chair to cut her hair while she screamed.

Zitkala-Sa spent a few years at the boarding school before she finally visited home. Her mother wanted her to stay, but she wanted to return to the school. Zitkala-Sa's time at the school had changed her. Many children sent to these schools shared her feelings and experiences. They forgot how to speak their language. They did not know a lot about their tribal ceremonies. They often felt they were no longer a part of their tribes, but they did not fit in with white people, either.

When Zitkala-Sa graduated from the boarding school in 1895, she went to Earlham College in Indiana. She wanted to be a teacher. There were not that many native students at Earlham. She left to enroll in the New England Conservatory of Music. She studied how to play the violin. Her education helped her get a job at Carlisle Indian Industrial School in 1900, where she taught speech and music. That school was located in Carlisle,

Pennsylvania, and was the first and most well-known Indian boarding school.

Zitkala-Sa worked there for only two years. She did not like that the government paid these schools for each native child they brought in. She watched as young children walked off the train and were forced to get their hair cut off. She also did not like how the staff were mean to the children.

She began writing about her experiences as well as the cultural values she learned from her mother. Many of her stories were published in magazines like the *Atlantic Monthly*. She published her writings in a book called *Old Indian Legends* in 1901.

Zitkala-Sa returned to South Dakota and got a job with the Bureau of Indian Affairs, which was a part of the US Department of the Interior. It made policies about land for native communities. She was able to support her family with the money from her job and wrote more stories about Dakota culture.

Zitkala-Sa also met her husband at the Bureau of Indian Affairs. His name was Raymond Talesfase Bonnin. She and Raymond got married in 1902. They had one son. His name was Raymond, too. They moved to the Utah reservation, where she got a job teaching native students. However, this was not a boarding school.

She met a music professor, William Hanson, who helped her bring together her music and writing. Shortly after meeting Hanson, she wrote an **opera** called *The Sun*

Dance. She was the first Native American to write an opera. The opera was based on her writings about her culture, so making an opera was another way for Zitkala-Sa to teach the culture with music.

Zitkala-Sa and her family moved to Washington, D.C., in 1916. She found a job with the Society of American Indians. She also worked for *American Indian Magazine*. Ten years later, she and her husband founded an organization called the National Council of American Indians. Zitkala-Sa also coordinated the Indian Welfare Committee. The committee studied living conditions on reservations. It also pressured the government to do a follow-up investigation, resulting in reforms in government policy.

Her employment with the Bureau of Indian Affairs began to make her unhappy. She wanted native culture to prosper, but the bureau was trying to erase it. Zitkala-Sa began creating awareness about native rights issues related to education, health, religion, and employment. Many native people on reservations could not find jobs, and their religion was outlawed.

The organizations Zitkala-Sa was a part of helped pass new laws, such as the 1924 Indian Citizenship Act, which provided US citizenship to Native Americans. Prior to this act, they were not recognized as US citizens. They could not vote and did not have a lot of rights.

Other committees she was a part of helped pass the Indian Reorganization Act of 1934. This law helped prevent the government from taking more land from Native

> ## "THERE IS NO GREAT; THERE IS NO SMALL; IN THE MIND THAT CAUSETH ALL."

Americans. It also helped promote native culture. During this time, native people could get into trouble if they performed tribal ceremonies. She felt these laws helped native people take back control over their lives.

Zitkala-Sa did not want her culture to disappear so native people could become "Americans." Most of her adult life was spent promoting native culture through her writing, music, and activism. Then, on January 26, 1938, Zitkala-Sa passed away in Washington, D.C.

Zitkala-Sa seemed to be ahead of her time. She wrote stories about her experiences in boarding schools during a time when most native people did not. She was able to transform her experiences into learning for others.

THINK IT THROUGH
During boarding school, Zitkala-Sa felt like she wasn't part of her tribe or part of white society. Have you ever felt like you weren't part of either one group or another? Did it change how you saw yourself?

EXPLORE MORE!
Learn more about the Carlisle Indian Industrial School, including the long-term impacts of the boarding school era on native people, at CarlisleIndianSchoolProject.com.

Jim
THORPE
{ 1888–1953 }

SAUK & FOX

Jim Thorpe has been described as the "world's greatest athlete," and for good reason. He won gold medals in the pentathlon and decathlon at the 1912 **Olympics** while wearing shoes he found in a garbage bin! Along with playing professional football and baseball, he was exceptional in other sports, too.

Jim was born in 1888 near Prague, Oklahoma, to Hiram and Charlotte Thorpe. His father was Sauk and Fox and half-Irish, and his mother was Citizen Band Potawatomie and French. When he was still a baby, he was named Wa-tho-huck, which means "Bright Path" in the Sauk and Fox language. He was a member of the Sauk & Fox Tribal Nation.

He grew up with his brothers and sisters on his father's farm, where he learned to hunt, shoot, ride and tame horses, and trap wild game. He had a twin brother named Charles, who unfortunately passed away from pneumonia when they were eight. His childhood was also disrupted when he was sent away to an Indian boarding school near Tecumseh, Oklahoma.

The children there were forced to live with strangers who were usually hostile to native culture. Jim ran away many times. He briefly attended the Haskell Institute in Lawrence, Kansas, then went to a public school after his mother's death in 1902.

Jim's father died from blood poisoning after Jim moved to Pennsylvania to attend the Carlisle Indian Industrial School. With his parents gone, Jim did not return to Oklahoma. He attended Carlisle off and on from 1904 to 1913. As a teenager nearing his twenties, he moved around and worked a lot.

Originally an army barracks, Carlisle was turned into the first Indian boarding school under Captain Richard Henry Pratt. For three years, Jim lived and worked with white families as part of Carlisle's "outing program." Instead of preparing native youth to **assimilate** into US society, as Pratt had boasted, the program actually turned the children into a cheap source of labor.

Carlisle is where Jim began to make a name for himself as a superb athlete. Shortly after leaving class one day, he jumped over a 5′9″ high bar on the athletic field. Amazingly, he accomplished this feat wearing his overalls. Legendary Coach Glenn "Pop" Warner saw this and informed Jim that he had just broken the school record for the high jump. Under Warner's guidance, Jim played 11 different sports for Carlisle. He especially excelled at football.

Carlisle competed against nearby teams, such as Harvard. In one game, Carlisle played against future US president Dwight D. Eisenhower. Newspapers praised Jim's athletic ability, calling him an uncatchable "shadow."

In 1911, Coach Warner encouraged Jim to participate in the 1912 Olympics in Stockholm, Sweden. Warner had been coaching him in track and field. His performance in Sweden is the legacy of his athletic career. Jim participated in the decathlon and pentathlon, which consisted of the **javelin** throw, disc throw, high jump, pole vault, and 200–1,500-meter races, among others. He won the gold medal while wearing mismatched shoes he found in the trash after his were stolen.

His record of 4 minutes and 40.2 seconds in the 1,500-meter run was not beaten until 1972. His record of 8,412 points in the decathlon was not broken for another 15 years. He won gold medals for the decathlon and pentathlon. Sweden's King Gustav V called him "the greatest athlete in the world," to which Jim replied, "Thanks, King."

A year later, the Olympic committee stripped Jim of his gold medals when they found out that he had played professional baseball between 1909 and 1910 in South Carolina. He said he hadn't been aware of the restrictions and didn't put up much of a fight over the decision.

After graduating from Carlisle in 1913, he married Iva Miller, and they had three daughters and one son together. Between 1913 and 1919, he played professional baseball with the New York Giants, Boston Braves, and Cincinnati

Reds. In 1920, Jim co-founded and became president of the American Professional Football Association, which would later become the **National Football League** (NFL).

Jim got remarried to Freeda Kirkpatrick in 1926, and they had four sons. After retiring from football in 1929, he moved to Hollywood. MGM bought the rights to his story, but they never made the film. He moved back to Oklahoma in 1937 and got involved in native issues, touring to give lectures on sports and native culture. In 1945, he remarried for the third and final time, to Patricia Askew.

In 1951, Jim's life story was made into a film starring Burt Lancaster. Jim served as a technical adviser. He was paid generously for his contribution. When a poll was taken in 1950, 400 sportswriters echoed the sentiments of King Gustav V and named Jim the greatest male athlete of the first half of the 20th century. In 1963, he was inducted into the Pro Football Hall of Fame.

But toward the end of his life, Jim struggled to make money to care for his children and worked various jobs. He was a stuntman in films, dug trenches, worked in construction, and was a security guard. In 1951, he developed lip cancer.

He never fought to get his gold medals reinstated. Although he was famous and tried to make a living off that fame, he never liked the attention.

Then, in 1953, at the age of 65, Jim passed away in Lomita, California. Despite his death, his legacy persists. And although the International Olympic Committee

> **"I HAVE ALWAYS LIKED SPORT AND ONLY PLAYED OR RUN RACES FOR THE FUN OF THE THING."**

reinstated his gold medals, providing his family with **replicas** in 1982, his 1912 Olympic record is still kept off the books. Regardless of what the Olympic committee has to say about his "official" performance, there is little doubt that generations of sports enthusiasts still view him as the greatest athlete that ever lived.

THINK IT THROUGH

Jim shrugged it off when his Olympic medals were taken away. Do you think he did the right thing? Would you have done the same thing he did?

EXPLORE MORE!

Learn more about Jim Thorpe, see photos of him, and read other famous quotes by and about him at CMGWW.com/sports/thorpe.

Maria
TALLCHIEF
{ 1925–2013 }
OSAGE

Maria Tallchief was a prima **ballerina** and became famous after her performance in George Balanchine's ballet *Firebird*. Despite facing prejudice for being an Osage woman, she raised awareness about native issues throughout her life.

Elizabeth Marie Tallchief was born on January 24, 1925, in Fairfax, Oklahoma, to Alexander J. Tallchief and Ruth Porter. Fairfax is located within the boundaries of the Osage reservation. Alexander was Osage and Ruth was Scotch Irish.

Maria, as she later came to be known, spent a lot of time with her grandmother, Eliza Big Heart Tallchief. Eliza taught Maria about her Osage culture and traditions. From an early age, Maria took a great interest in dance, as did her sister, Marjorie. Maria's family was able to afford dance lessons due to oil headrights. A headright was money given to Osage people for access to oil on their land. Her great-grandfather, Pete Big Heart, helped secure oil money on Osage lands in 1906.

As a young girl, Maria was known as Betty Marie. Aside from her sister, Marjorie, she also had one brother, Gerald. When she was eight, she moved to Los Angeles, California. Her mother encouraged her interest in music, hoping she would become a pianist. Although she was musically talented, her main focus was dance, which her mother supported as well. Maria began lessons with Bronislava Nijinska, a **renowned** Polish ballerina. Later, she took ballet classes with Tatiana Riabouchinska, a Russian classical dancer and instructor.

High school students mocked Tallchief with racist comments. They made fun of her last name, said her father scalped people, and hollered war whoops in front of her. When she and Marjorie danced at county fairs, they were forced to perform in buckskin and feathers. White audiences wanted to see authentic Indian dances. However, these dances were not an accurate depiction of Osage culture.

After graduating from high school, Maria moved to New York City to dedicate herself to her dance career. That career began slowly, as many studios told her they had no room for her. But Maria refused to give up. She auditioned for the Ballet Russe de Monte Carlo in 1942 and became an **understudy**. That same year, she was called to take over for another dancer who had quit. Maria performed in ballets such as *Les Sylphides* and *Rodeo.* She received outstanding reviews and was praised for her precision and strength.

Two years later, she landed a role in the opera *Song of Norway,* choreographed by George Balanchine. Balanchine was regarded as a ballet "master" **choreographer** and furthered Maria's dance career with more opportunities in *Ballet Imperial* and *Le Baiser de la Fée.* Eventually, Balanchine asked Maria to marry him. She accepted, and their wedding took place in August 1946.

The two moved to France and started working for the Paris Opera Ballet. Maria was the first American to be a part of this dance troupe. After returning to the United States, Balanchine started the New York City Ballet in 1948. Maria was one of the first dancers to star in the new ballet company. She played the swan queen in *Swan Lake* and the Sugar Plum Fairy in *The Nutcracker.* She also played the lead role in *Firebird,* a story about a prince and a mythical firebird, which is based on Russian **folklore**. Her performance in this famed work choreographed by Balanchine brought her a lot of attention.

Maria had become successful as a prima ballerina but still faced discrimination. Dance companies wanted her to change her last name to "Tallchieva." She refused, but she did change her first name to Maria instead of going by her birth name, Elizabeth. When she traveled to France, newspaper headlines stated, "Redskin Dances at the Opera." Because of her faithfulness to her Osage heritage and success in American ballet, her Osage community gave Maria a new name—Wa-xthe-thonba. It means "Woman of Two Worlds" or "Woman of Two Standards."

Maria and Balanchine separated in 1951 but remained working partners in the New York City Ballet. Maria was married twice afterward. She was with Elmourza Natirboff from 1952 to 1954. Her third and final marriage was to Henry "Buzz" Paschen. They had one daughter together, Elise Maria Paschen. Elise was her only child.

In 1954, Maria was the highest-paid prima ballerina. She earned $2,000 a week. Today, that is roughly $19,000 per week.

After retiring from dancing in 1965, Maria remained dedicated to ballet and advocated for more native participation in the arts. Maria and Marjorie opened a dance studio called the Chicago City Ballet. As a well-respected and world-renowned prima ballerina, Maria set an example of what native people could accomplish and overcome.

Maria won many honors and awards in her lifetime. In 1953, the State of Oklahoma declared June 29 Maria Tallchief Day. Between 1973 and 1979, she was the director of Chicago's Lyric Opera Ballet. In 1991, she and her sister, Marjorie, who also became a renowned ballerina, were included in the *Flight of Spirit* mural in the Oklahoma State Capitol. In 1996, she received the Kennedy Center Honors award for contributing to the arts. That same year, she was inducted into the National Women's Hall of Fame. The US government awarded her the National Medal of Arts in 1999.

> **"IF ANYTHING AT ALL, PERFECTION IS NOT WHEN THERE IS NOTHING TO ADD, BUT WHEN THERE IS NOTHING LEFT TO TAKE AWAY."**

Maria passed away at the age of 88 on April 11, 2013. Her contributions to the world of ballet demonstrated her resolve in the face of hardship. She never allowed discrimination to stop her from pursuing her dream. In refusing to change her last name and advocating for her community, she set an example for other indigenous women and the native community as a whole to remain true to who they are.

THINK IT THROUGH

Why was it important for Maria Tallchief to stay true to her Osage heritage? Have you ever struggled to stay true to something when it would have been easier not to?

EXPLORE MORE!

You can learn more about Maria's cultural traditions and history, as well her tribe's effort to preserve their ways, at OsageNation-NSN.gov.

Susan
LaFLESCHE

{ *1865–1915* }

OMAHA

Susan LaFlesche was the first Native American woman to become a doctor. She provided medical care to the Omaha Nation people on their reservation. She opened a clinic that served native and non-native people. Susan also worked to improve the lives of native people by educating them about diseases.

Susan was born in Nebraska on the Omaha Reservation on June 17, 1865. Her parents were Joseph and Mary LaFlesche. Her father, known as Iron Eye, was a community leader and the last recognized chief of the Omaha tribe.

It was a **tumultuous** time, as the old ways were fading away. The US government was forcing native people onto reservations and taking more of their land. Native traditions were banned. The world the Omaha knew was changing forever. Susan's father felt that embracing white American values such as education was a way to survive.

As a teenager, Susan was sent to New Jersey to attend the Elizabeth Institute for Young Ladies. She returned to the reservation at the age of 17 and taught at the **Quaker** Mission School. She met Alice Fletcher not long after her return. Alice was a notable woman in the field of **anthropology**. She was an intellectual and an active supporter of **social justice** and women's rights. Alice had studied the lives of Native Americans with Frederic W. Putnam. He was in charge of the Peabody Museum at Harvard University.

Alice started working at the Omaha mission school in 1880. Unfortunately, she became sick and needed care. Susan stayed by her side and helped nurse her back to health. Alice was very grateful for Susan's help. She encouraged Susan to get a college education and go to medical school.

Eventually, Susan enrolled at the Hampton Normal and Agricultural Institute in Virginia. Hampton was a **trade school** for Native Americans and African Americans. The school was considered one of the best for the instruction of non-white students. Her dedication to school was also motivated by a horrible incident she witnessed as a child. She watched as a local white doctor refused to provide medical care to a sick and dying Omaha woman. This made her want to help provide health care to the Omaha community.

In 1886, Susan graduated from Hampton second in her class. She then enrolled in the Women's Medical College of Pennsylvania. More schooling required more money.

Alice Fletcher helped Susan collect the money she needed through the US Office of Indian Affairs.

Susan was going to medical school at a time when white American women were treated very poorly in American society. White American men published science articles suggesting that women had "small brains." They did not want women in college because they said the stress would cause them child-bearing problems. This type of discrimination was very common. For Susan, an *Omaha* woman, going to medical school during this time was extremely unusual and remarkable.

Susan graduated in 1889, a year early and at the top of her class. She completed a yearlong internship in Philadelphia and then returned to the Omaha Reservation. There, she was able to provide medical care to an estimated 1,200 people. She was persistent in her job. She often walked for miles to help sick Omaha people who lived far away.

Sometimes, it was blisteringly cold and snowing. If she was lucky, she would ride to patients' homes on a horse. She eventually got a buggy. Unfortunately, after traveling far to see her patients, some Omaha people rejected her **diagnosis** because they were suspicious of her "white schooling."

Susan's work was very demanding. Omaha people piled in looking for help with cholera and tuberculosis. Often, they also asked for her help with issues not related to medicine, like legal and financial problems. When her white co-worker suddenly quit, Susan became the only doctor on a reservation that stretched for more than 1,300 miles.

In 1894, she married Henry Picotte, a Lakota from South Dakota. They moved to Bancroft, Nebraska, where Susan established a private practice tending to both non-white and white patients. Her work was still hectic, but she managed to raise two boys.

She worked to support laws that prevented the sale of alcohol on reservations. Many Omaha people, including her husband, struggled with alcohol abuse. She witnessed the destruction alcohol caused up close. Henry's alcohol addiction made it difficult for him to heal when he was diagnosed with tuberculosis. He eventually died from the disease.

In 1913, Susan opened a hospital on the reservation in the town of Walthill. She continued to have a very busy schedule. When she was 40 years old, she went deaf in one ear. Her loss of hearing was caused by an unknown chronic illness. Despite her own health problems, Susan continued to help the Omaha people as best she could, educating them about diseases like tuberculosis and influenza. She also testified in Washington, D.C., about Omaha lands still being taken from her people.

Susan's hard work and dedication eventually paid off. In 1913, she opened the *first* privately funded hospital on an Indian reservation. Unfortunately, she was not able to enjoy her success for long. She passed away from bone cancer on September 18, 1915, at the age of 50. Her funeral represented the two worlds she wanted to bridge together. Catholic priests provided a **eulogy** and an Omaha elder said prayers in their native language. After her death, the hospital was renamed the *Dr. Susan LaFlesche Picotte Memorial Hospital*. The hospital served the community for 30 years. Today, it is a historical landmark.

Susan showed how determination and a will to continue can lead to great things. She went to medical school and overcame the odds against her as a Native American woman during a time when neither women in general nor indigenous people were viewed as equals in white society. Her life was full of challenges, but she continued to help and heal native and non-native people.

THINK IT THROUGH
Susan was the first Native American woman to become a doctor. What challenges come from being first at something? Can you think of any benefits?

EXPLORE MORE!
Learn about the Omaha Tribe of Nebraska's history, culture, and present at www.OmahaTribe.com.

Bertha
PARKER CODY
{ 1907–1978 }
SENECA

Bertha Parker Cody was the first Native American woman **archaeologist**. She had no formal training, but became an expert by working directly in the field. She was also able to influence the way non-natives view native people by advocating for accurate depictions in film and media.

Bertha Parker Cody was born in a tent at the Silverheels **excavation site** in Cattaraugus County, New York. The project was led by her father, Arthur C. Parker. Her mother was Beulah Tahamont. Arthur was Seneca and Beulah was Abenaki. Bertha also went by Yewas, her Seneca name, and by the nickname Bertie.

Bertha's dad was an archaeologist, historian, and **musicologist**. He was also the president of the Society for American Archaeology. Archaeologists study human history by finding and examining artifacts. Her great uncle, Ely S. Parker, was the first native commissioner for Indian affairs.

After Bertha's parents separated in 1914, she moved to Los Angeles, California, with her mother and grandparents. Bertha's maternal grandparents and mother were actors. As a child, Bertha performed with her mother in the Ringling Brothers and Barnum and Bailey Circus's *Pocahontas* show. This was about the myth of Pocahontas saving John Smith's life before he was about to be killed by her father, Powhatan.

In 1925, Bertha married Joseph Pallan, who worked as an extra in movies. They had one daughter, named Wilma Mae. Wilma Mae also went by Billie. Unfortunately, Joseph became abusive to Bertha. He kidnapped her and their daughter and drove to Mexico. Bertha's uncle, Mark Raymond Harrington, came to rescue her. Bertha then divorced her husband.

Her uncle worked as an archaeologist. He let Bertha and her daughter live with him and his wife. He hired Bertha to cook and to be his secretary. She participated in excavations and learned about archaeological methods. She had no formal schooling and learned everything from experience.

Bertha was helping dig up **artifacts** at a place called Mesa House when she found an ancient Pueblo village. She called it Scorpion Hill. Her reports on Scorpion Hill were later published. Some of the artifacts were put on display in the Southwest Museum of the American Indian in Los Angeles.

Bertha also worked with her uncle in Nevada at a site called Gypsum Cave. The cave contained artifacts of some of the first human beings in North America.

Bertha's job was to organize what they found. She also discovered another archaeological site nearby, where she found a camel bone sticking up out of the ground in a partially dry lake bed.

She continued to explore Gypsum Cave, where she found **prehistoric** tools and a skull from an extinct species of giant sloth. The sloth skull led the California Institute of Technology to provide additional funding for their research.

Bertha's uncle hired a **paleontologist** named James Thurston. James and Bertha fell in love and got married in 1931. Sadly, a year later, James got sick and died from a heart attack at 27 years of age. Bertha got very sick, too. She moved from Nevada back to Los Angeles. Their sickness may have been caused by the air at one of the archaeological sites.

Bertha went on to publish many papers on archaeology and **ethnology** over the next 40 years. While archeology involves the study of human history through discovery and analysis of artifacts and biological remains, ethnology looks at the characteristics of different peoples and their connections to one another. Bertha wrote about Kachina dolls and Yurok baby baskets. Kachina dolls were made by the Hopi and represented helpful spirits from the underworld. Yurok baby baskets were woven together with plant fibers such as hazel, willow, and conifer root. They were used to carry babies.

In 1936, Bertha married a man named Espera Oscar de Corti. He was a movie actor who went by the stage name

"Iron Eyes Cody." Espera was an unusual person. He was Italian but told people he was part Cherokee. Bertha and Espera adopted two Native American children after Bertha's daughter, Wilma Mae, was accidentally killed from a gunshot wound when she was 17.

Bertha then found work as an adviser for television shows in the 1940s. An adviser helps make the movie or show more truthful. Her job influenced the way Native American culture and history were shown on television and on the big screen. Espera and Bertha hosted a show in the 1950s that taught people about native history. They also helped native people who recently moved to California get support from the Los Angeles Indian Center. The center provided a place where native people could socialize.

Even though Bertha did a lot to promote native people in Hollywood and through archaeology, she is not very well known outside the field of archaeology. Most writings about her simply describe her based on the men she was around. Bertha passed away in 1978 at the age of 71. Her tombstone does not have her name on it. Instead, it says "Mrs. Iron Eyes Cody."

Bertha's legacy as the first Native American woman archaeologist is important to learn. She contributed a lot to the field of archaeology. She did this with respect for the people and cultures she was studying. When she interviewed other native people about their culture, she wrote down their names and credited them as co-authors. Her care in recognizing the people in the community

> "BERTHA CODY WAS AN OUTSTANDING EXAMPLE OF A SELF-TAUGHT TALENT, SHOWING HOW 'FORMAL' EDUCATION IS NOT THE WAY EVERYBODY LEARNS AND THAT PRACTICAL EXPERIENCE CAN LEAD TO EXCELLENT WORK. MUCH OF THE EDUCATION AVAILABLE TO BERTHA DURING HER LIFE STEMMED DIRECTLY FROM RACISM AND COLONIALISM AND WAS A FORM OF CULTURAL GENOCIDE."
>
> —POC Squared

makes her a great example for others who have an interest in archaeology or other fields of knowledge.

~~~~~~

THINK IT THROUGH
How did Bertha Parker's Seneca background impact the way she wrote about other Native Americans?

EXPLORE MORE!
Want to learn more about the Abenaki Tribe today, including its culture and traditions? Visit AbenakiTribe.org.

Vine
DELORIA JR.
{ 1933–2005 }
DAKOTA

Vine Deloria Jr. was a professor, writer, speaker, and **activist**. He was the author, co-author, or editor of 25 books. His most popular book is *Custer Died for Your Sins: An Indian Manifesto,* published in 1969. Vine Jr.'s literary contributions and advocacy for a better world are still inspiring to people today.

Vine Victor Deloria Jr. was born in Martin, South Dakota, on March 26, 1933. Martin is a small town next to the Pine Ridge Indian Reservation. His father was Vine Deloria Sr. and his mother was Barbara S. Eastburn. Vine Jr. had two younger siblings, Philip and Barbara.

Vine Jr. came from a long line of spiritual leaders. His great-grandfather was Saswe, a Dakota spiritual leader. The Deloria family became Episcopalians after Saswe had a series of visions that led him to follow Christianity. Saswe's son, Tipi Sapa, and grandson, Vine Sr., became Episcopalian priests. Vine Sr. believed Dakota spirituality was similar to Christianity because both have rules for how to treat people.

As a boy, Vine Jr. traveled with his father to different native communities. Vine Sr. was a missionary who taught people about Christianity and the Bible. Vine Jr. and his father went to church services *and* **traditional** Dakota ceremonies.

When Vine Jr. was 16 years old, he moved to Connecticut and attended Kent School, a private preparatory school. After he graduated from Kent, he enrolled in the Colorado School of Mines. He wrote on his application that he wanted to become a **geologist** out of respect for his ancestors, who once owned the land. Vine Jr. wanted to help native people make better decisions about how to use the land. However, he didn't do too well in geology school and dropped out.

He then attended Iowa State University for a little while. He felt uninspired, left school again, and enlisted in the US Marines. He served from 1954 to 1956 as a telephone repairman. The Marines helped him earn money for college, and he re-enrolled in Iowa State to pursue a general science degree. It was there that he met his wife, Barbara Jeanne Nystrom. They both graduated in 1958 and had three children together: Philip, Daniel, and Jeanne.

Vine Jr. moved around to different schools and jobs to support his family. He briefly attended the University of Oregon for a master's degree, then left. Then he moved to Chicago to find work. He got a job in Puerto Rico teaching

English at a religious school for three months. Afterward, he enrolled in the Lutheran School of Theology and earned a master's degree in theology, the study of religions.

Vine Jr. served as the director of the National Congress of American Indians (NCAI) between 1964 and 1967. The NCAI serves the interests of native communities and tribal governments. He was its main spokesperson and testified before the US Congress to help improve civil rights for Native Americans. He advocated for letting tribal communities control the education of their own children using indigenous knowledge. He argued that native knowledge is just as important as non-native knowledge.

His experiences with the NCAI motivated him to attend law school. He thought one way to help his people was to understand federal law. He enrolled in Colorado Law School in 1967. During that time, he helped raise his family and wrote his most well-known book, *Custer Died for Your Sins: An Indian Manifesto*. It was published in 1969, just before he graduated with his law degree in 1970. The book was a huge success.

Vine Jr. wanted the US government and Christian leaders to quit interfering in native lives. He also wrote about his dislike for anthropology, which he thought was too invasive.

Vine Jr. later taught political science at the University of Arizona. While there, he started the first-ever master's degree program in American Indian Studies. Native and non-native students could now further their education about indigenous social issues, history, law, education, and current events.

In 1997, Vine Jr. became involved in the Kennewick Man debate. "Kennewick Man" was the name given to skeletal remains found near the town of Kennewick, Washington. They were estimated to be around 10,000 years old. Local tribes wanted Kennewick Man to be reburied with a proper ceremony. Scientists claimed they had a right to study the remains. The scientists were allowed to study them for a short time.

Scientists issued a report stating Kennewick Man hunted and gathered wild foods to eat. They also said Kennewick Man was "handsome" and had good health. To Vine Jr., it seemed ridiculous that scientists claimed the skeletal remains were "handsome." He was concerned that the scientists were making things up.

Vine Jr. also argued against the Bering Strait Theory. This theory says Native Americans came to North America by crossing a land bridge from Asia. If scientists claim that Native Americans were not always in North America, then the government could deny native land claims. Vine Jr. explores this idea in one of his other books called *Red Earth, White Lies*.

Vine Jr.'s writings always supported the right of native people to determine their own future. He advocated for the right of tribes to create their own laws. He appeared on many documentaries and television shows to discuss native rights. Vine Jr. was described by *Time* magazine as one of the 20th century's most important religious

> **"RELIGION, AS I HAVE EXPERIENCED IT, IS NOT THE RECITATION OF BELIEFS, BUT A WAY OF HELPING TO UNDERSTAND OUR LIVES."**

thinkers. His last published book was *The World We Used to Live In: Remembering the Powers of the Medicine Men*.

Vine Jr. passed away at the age of 72 on November 13, 2005, in Golden, Colorado. Many people remember him as a strong voice for native people. As a writer and scholar, Vine Jr. showed people what you can accomplish when you devote your time to spreading truth. His legacy in the fields of religious thinking and native politics will continue to inspire generations to come.

THINK IT THROUGH

Do you think scientists had the right to study the Kennewick Man or do you think the remains should have been immediately given to the local tribes to rebury?

EXPLORE MORE!

Learn about the Lakota Dakota Nakota Nation and its values of balance, harmony, abundance, and peace at LakotaDakotaNakotaNation.org.

Russell
CHARLES MEANS
{ 1939–2012 }
OGLALA LAKOTA

Russell Means was a leader of the American Indian Movement, an actor, and an advocate for native rights. He constantly spoke up against the injustices faced by indigenous people. He is best known for leading the Wounded Knee standoff with the US government in 1973.

Russell Charles Means was born on November 10, 1939, on the Pine Ridge Indian Reservation in South Dakota. His parents were Walter and Theodora Louise Feather Means. Russell was their first-born child. Altogether, he had three brothers and three sisters.

As a child, Russell spent a lot of time with his grandfather, who taught him about Lakota culture. They would go on long walks in the countryside. Grandpa John taught Russell to have respect for the land and shared valuable life lessons with him.

Russell's mother gave him the Lakota name Wanbli Ohitika, which means "Brave Eagle." Grandpa John told him that Lakota people earn four names during their life. The first name is given when they are born, and the second one is given in childhood. The third name is received as an adult, and the fourth one is given in old age. His grandma, Twinkle Star, also taught him about their family history.

When Russell was in elementary school, he was told he would not amount to anything. He was accused of giving his white classmates lice, but when they checked his hair, he didn't have any. He also got into a fight with a white student who was bullying him. Russell's parents moved their family to Vallejo, California, in 1942. His mother wanted her children to have better opportunities than what the reservation could offer. There weren't very many jobs on Pine Ridge. During the summers, he would return to South Dakota to stay with his grandparents, aunts, and uncles. One summer, he was almost drowned by other kids.

Russell's father was a welder and worked at a Navy shipyard in Vallejo. He struggled with alcoholism. Sometimes, Russell's mother asked him to search for his dad at the local bars. One time, while walking around town looking for their dad, his younger siblings were picked up by the police.

Russell did well in elementary and middle school. When he went to high school, his home life became tougher. His dad was always at the bars, and his mom worked long hours. Russell didn't get a lot of emotional or academic support from his parents during that time. He began to skip school and would get suspended. One time, he was arrested for stealing beer with his friends. Despite these problems, Russell graduated from San Leandro High School in 1958.

Russell eventually married his first wife, Betty Means, and they had two children. Although he enrolled in four different colleges, he never graduated and jumped from job to job. When he moved the family to Cleveland, Ohio, he worked with the Cleveland American Indian Center. He became more involved in native civil rights.

Russell met Dennis Banks and Vernon Bellecourt in 1969. Banks and Bellecourt had created a group called the American Indian Movement (AIM) in Minneapolis, Minnesota. AIM wanted more native people to learn about their culture and traditions in the 1960s and 1970s. It also helped native people get jobs. The organization founded the Heart of the Earth Survival School, which helps native children learn about their culture. The school is still around today.

Russell joined AIM when he was 30 years old. He was a good speaker and helped bring a lot of attention to AIM and Native American causes. In 1970, during Thanksgiving, he led AIM activists onto a replica of the *Mayflower* ship near Plymouth Rock, Massachusetts. They were protesting the United States' mistreatment of indigenous people. The police showed up, convincing them to leave.

Russell became famous for leading the Wounded Knee takeover of 1973. Wounded Knee was where the US cavalry killed 300 unarmed Lakota women, children, and men in 1890. This site was an important symbol of the country's treatment of Lakota people. AIM was invited by the Lakota community to help bring attention to problems on the Pine Ridge Indian Reservation. They wanted the tribal chairman to leave, claiming he was harming his own people. AIM also wanted the US government to better help native communities.

Russell gave many speeches during the takeover. He told news reporters that the US government needed to uphold treaty rights. Treaty rights were promises the US government made to help native communities with things like health care and education to make up for taking their lands. The government did not keep many of these promises, and this upset many Native Americans.

AIM members and supporters came to Wounded Knee with guns. They were surrounded by the US Federal Bureau of Investigation, US Marshals Service, and other police agencies. The two sides shot at each other. The takeover ended after 71 days. Two native men were killed, and a marshal was paralyzed. Russell was arrested and sent to jail for his role in the incident, but his case was dismissed.

Russell left AIM in the 1980s but continued to support native rights. He protested Columbus Day and condemned the use of Indian **mascots** by sports teams. He also became an actor, co-starring in the 1992 movie

> "TRADITIONALLY, AMERICAN INDIANS HAVE ALWAYS ATTEMPTED TO BE THE BEST PEOPLE THEY COULD. PART OF THAT SPIRITUAL PROCESS WAS AND IS TO GIVE AWAY WEALTH, TO DISCARD WEALTH IN ORDER NOT TO GAIN."

The Last of the Mohicans. He continued to play small roles in movies and television. His autobiography, titled *Where White Men Fear to Tread,* was published in 1995.

Russell passed away from throat cancer on October 22, 2012, at his home outside Porcupine, South Dakota. He was 72. He lived a long life that inspired younger generations. He always spoke his mind and advocated for his community. Russell will be remembered by many people as a courageous man who devoted his life to creating change.

THINK IT THROUGH
What might have gone differently in Russell Means's life if he had received better support from his parents?

EXPLORE MORE!
Want to learn more about the Oglala Lakota Nation, including its programs and constitution? Visit OglalaLakotaNation.info.

Wilma
PEARL MANKILLER
{ 1945–2010 }

CHEROKEE

Wilma Mankiller was the first woman to become principal chief of the Cherokee Nation. She sought to improve the tribe's education and health care services. She worked to bring her community together and overcome the poverty that impacted Cherokee people. Her position brought back the tradition of women providing the core leadership for Cherokee people.

Wilma Pearl Mankiller was born on November 18, 1945, in Tahlequah, Oklahoma. Her parents were Charley and Irene Mankiller. She was the sixth of eleven children. Her father was Cherokee, and her mother was Irish and Dutch. The name "Mankiller" is the English translation of the Cherokee word *Asgaya-dihi*. "Mankiller" was a title a Cherokee had to earn. It is like calling someone in the US Army a "captain."

As a child, Wilma was teased in school because of her name. But her parents taught her to be proud of it. Wilma always talked about wanting to honor her ancestors, who shared her last name, by keeping it alive.

Growing up, Wilma lived in a small house with a lot of family members. Her father and uncles built the home. It had a tin roof and the floors were bare wood. Her family used a wood stove for cooking and for keeping the house warm during the winter. They did not have a bathroom and had to use an **outhouse**. Instead of a refrigerator, they used a box placed in cold water to keep milk and other foods cool. As a kid, she had to wear a flour sack as underwear because they were so poor.

Wilma's Cherokee ancestors came from Tennessee and were called "Old Settlers." The Old Settler Cherokees moved voluntarily a few years before the remaining Cherokees were forced to leave on the Trail of Tears—a death march enacted by President Andrew Jackson. He wanted all native people to move west of the Mississippi River. Wilma grew up in Adair County, Oklahoma, listening to her parents speak Cherokee and English.

When Wilma was a child, she would attend the Cherokee green corn ceremony. It was a way for the Cherokee to give thanks to the creator for growing corn. The ceremony was a time of rebirth. Her family also planted and harvested food such as wild onions, mushrooms, and berries. They made extra money by growing and selling strawberries and peanuts. Wilma always had enough food to eat, even though her family was poor.

Wilma's father struggled to earn money. He eventually moved the family to California when Wilma was about 11.

But the family also endured a lot of discrimination there. One time, a white lady called her family racist names in public. Her mother was so upset that she attacked the woman.

Wilma's family lived in a poor neighborhood in the San Francisco Bay Area. There was a lot of crime and drug use, and gangs were common. Wilma didn't like living in a city or going to a new school. She and her siblings had Oklahoma accents, and the other kids made fun of how they talked. She felt alone. Wilma loved her family, but was becoming more independent. Her father worked all the time, and her mother was taking care of 11 children.

She started running away to her grandmother's house at the age of 12. She felt more comfortable there. Eventually, her parents agreed to let her live with Grandma Sitton for one year. Grandma Sitton lived with Wilma's aunt, uncle, and cousins on a dairy ranch. They woke up very early to milk the cows each day. Sometimes, Wilma fought with her cousins. After a year, she moved back home. She visited every summer until Grandma Sitton passed away.

After she graduated high school, Wilma started hanging out at the American Indian Center. She got involved in politics and supported the **civil rights movement** for African Americans. In 1963, she got married to Hugo Olaya and had two daughters.

In 1969, she was inspired by the takeover of **Alcatraz Island** near San Francisco. Hundreds of Native American activists occupied the island and demanded the US government "give it back" to native people. They also wanted Alcatraz to become a cultural center. Wilma went to the island with some of her brothers and sisters. The experience motivated her to do more to help native people.

In 1977, she got a divorce and moved back to Oklahoma with her daughters. Then, two years later, she got into a head-on collision while driving to the Cherokee Nation headquarters. She almost died. She spent one year recovering. However, soon after her recovery, she was diagnosed with myasthenia gravis, a neuromuscular disease that made it difficult for her to speak and use her hands. These two incidents were challenging, but they made her want to do more with her life.

She started helping the Cherokee tribal government, and in 1983, she became the deputy chief of the Cherokee. Then, in 1985, she became chief of the Cherokee Nation. She was elected twice more in 1987 and 1991. She served as Cherokee chief until 1995.

Wilma oversaw a Cherokee membership of 140,000. She managed a $75 million budget and opened health centers and a Head Start program for Cherokee children. The program offers services that help kids succeed in school. In 1986, she got married to another Cherokee man. He was named Charlie Soap. Despite her health problems, she continued to speak and write. In 1993, she published her autobiography, *Mankiller: A Chief and Her People*.

On April 6, 2010, Wilma Mankiller passed away from pancreatic cancer, but not before leaving a lasting legacy.

> **"THE SECRET OF OUR SUCCESS IS THAT WE NEVER, NEVER GIVE UP."**

Wilma always recognized the need for native people to stay rooted to their heritage and solve their own problems. Despite experiencing tragedies with her health and relationships, she continued to move forward, demonstrating what a person can accomplish while facing the challenges life can bring.

THINK IT THROUGH

How did Wilma Mankiller's last name help her stay connected to her heritage and remain proud of her roots?

EXPLORE MORE!

Ever wanted to learn a second language? The Cherokee Nation's website offers language classes and more. Check it out at Cherokee.org.

Suzan
SHOWN HARJO

{ 1945–Present }

MUSCOGEE CREEK-CHEYENNE

Suzan Harjo is a Muscogee Creek-Cheyenne poet, writer, and social justice activist. For years, she has raised awareness about Native American issues. She has taken the lead in helping create laws and policies that protect tribal traditions, artifacts, and sacred sites. She is best known for filing a lawsuit against the Washington Redskins football team (now the Washington Football Team) to force them to change their name.

Suzan was born in El Reno, Oklahoma, on June 2, 1945. Her parents were Freeland and Susie Douglas. Freeland was Muscogee-Creek, and Susie was Cheyenne. Suzan's family background includes fighters and warriors. Her great-grandfather was Chief Bull Bear, a well-known leader of the Cheyenne Dog Soldiers Society. Dog Soldiers were Cheyenne warriors who wanted white American settlers out of their territory.

Suzan's dad was a World War II veteran and traveled to different bases around the world. Suzan, her mother, and her brothers stayed with her grandparents while he was away. However, they would join their father when he was stationed in Hawai'i or Italy.

Suzan endured anti-native racism and abuse. These experiences made her want to change the world in a positive way. Some of her mentors were spiritual leaders and teachers who taught her to be prepared to speak, lead, and follow. Her work as a community leader was influenced by a Cheyenne teaching that says, "The nation shall be strong so long as the hearts of the women are not on the ground."

Suzan's Muscogee-Creek ancestors were from present-day Alabama, but were forced to move west in the 1800s by President Andrew Jackson's Indian Removal Act that forced native people to move west. She has harvested traditional plant medicines in the southeastern United States as a way to reconnect with her Muscogee culture.

Suzan started working on **repatriation** in 1965 during a trip to the Museum of the American Indian in New York City. Repatriation is the act of returning ceremonial items held by museums. Many museums in the United States keep objects dug up from burial sites of native people. They also keep the skeletons of native people's ancestors. Her mother noticed the museum had clothes she helped make for her grandfather to be buried in when he passed away. There was also a buckskin dress with a bullet hole in it that belonged to a Cheyenne girl. Suzan's mother told her those items were sacred and should be reburied.

Suzan was also a producer and co-host for a New York City radio program called *Seeing Red* in 1967. It was the first radio broadcast show that discussed native issues. She worked on this show with her husband, Frank Harjo, whom she met in New York City. He was also from the Muscogee-Creek tribe. They interviewed Native American students about how they were treated in school. They also interviewed American Indian Movement leaders Russell Means and Dennis Banks.

In 1974, they moved to Washington, D.C., where Suzan worked with two law firms that took cases involving native rights. Her legal efforts helped return control of more than one million acres of land to tribes such as the Lakota, Cheyenne, and Zuni.

She also helped create the 1978 American Indian Religious Freedom Act, which enables Native Americans to access sacred sites and legally possess eagle feathers for ceremonies. Many states had established "no trespassing" laws on land where sacred sites are located. If native people went onto these lands to pray, they could be arrested. Also, it was illegal for people to own eagle feathers, which are used in some native ceremonies. Suzan's work helped reverse these policies for native people.

In 1989, she drafted the National Museum of the American Indian Act. This act included some of the first protections for Native American burial remains. The Native American Graves Protection and Repatriation Act was passed shortly afterward in 1990. It forces museums that get their money from the government to return ceremonial objects and skeletal remains to local tribes. The museums also have to tell the tribes what kinds of native artifacts they have.

In 1992, Suzan helped file a lawsuit against the Washington football team formerly known as the "Redskins." The term was used in an 1863 Minnesota newspaper advertisement that promised a $200 reward for every "redskin sent to **purgatory**." Native Americans felt the team's name supported violence against native people. In July 2020, the team officially stopped using the name. Suzan has written many essays addressing the Indian mascot problem, with titles such as "Fighting Name-Calling: Challenging 'Redskins' in Court" and "Just Good Sports: The Impact of 'Native' References in Sports on Native Youth and What Some Decolonizers Have Done About It."

Suzan is the president of the Morning Star Institute, which continues to promote returning land to tribes and protecting native religious freedom. She created the Morning Star Institute to honor her husband shortly after he passed away.

She has also written many opinion articles for the Native American–owned newspaper *Indian Country Today* and was the director of the American Indian Press Association. In 2000, she was the keynote speaker at an event for the UNITY: Journalists of Color association. That association was created to improve news coverage of Native American, African American, Asian American, and Hispanic communities.

> **"POETRY APPEALS TO ME BECAUSE IT CAN HAVE THE GRACE OF WATER AND THE FOCUS OF ROCK..."**

Suzan's poetry has appeared in many poetry journals, such as the *New York Quarterly, Potomac Review,* and *Antaeus.* A compilation of her poetry was published with the title *Blood of the Sun: Artists Respond to the Poetry of Suzan Shown Harjo.*

In 2014, President Barack Obama awarded Suzan the Presidential Medal of Freedom. Obama said, "Because of Suzan, more young Native Americans are growing up with pride in their heritage and with faith in their future." His statement describes her impact for the past 40 years.

THINK IT THROUGH
What does "The nation shall be strong so long as the hearts of the women are not on the ground" mean to you? What did it mean to Suzan?

EXPLORE MORE!
Did you know that the Muscogee Creek Nation is the fourth-largest Native American tribe in the United States? Visit its website at MCN-NSN.gov to learn about its culture, heritage, and language.

John
BENNETT HERRINGTON
{ 1958–Present }
CHICKASAW

John Herrington was the first Native American astronaut to visit space. He trained as a US Navy pilot and was accepted into the National Aeronautics and Space Administration (NASA) space program. After retiring, he has lectured and taught about his experiences with flying and space travel. He encourages young people to continue their education so they can pursue their dreams.

John was born in Wetumka, Oklahoma, on September 14, 1958, to James and Joyce Herrington. He lived in Wyoming, Texas, and Colorado before he was a high school senior. He moved a total of 14 times.

As a kid, John took flying lessons with his dad. His dad was a flight instructor, and they visited a lot of air shows. He was fascinated by NASA's space program in the 1960s. He dreamed of becoming a pilot and one day going to space.

John's parents encouraged him to get an education, and he enrolled at the University of Colorado. He spent a lot of time rock climbing instead of going to his classes, and eventually, he was expelled from the school. John's climbing hobby helped him find a job with a land survey crew as a climber, carrying equipment up steep terrain. It was during this time that he discovered he was actually good at math. His supervisor encouraged him to go back to school. John did just that.

He enrolled once again at the University of Colorado. This time, his experience was more rewarding. He found a close group of friends and created a study group. He also became a math tutor. One of the students he tutored was a former Navy captain who talked about flying for a living. This inspired John to pursue his goal of becoming a pilot. In 1983, he graduated with an applied mathematics degree.

He then enlisted in the Navy and became a naval aviator in 1985, flying a total of 3,300 hours in 30 different kinds of planes. He was also a test pilot and a flight instructor. During this time, he realized he might really become an astronaut, as all the astronauts he admired had been Navy pilots.

John improved his chances of becoming an astronaut by getting an aeronautical engineering degree from the US Naval Postgraduate School. He was selected along with 44 other candidates to begin astronaut training with NASA in 1996.

He started out assisting with NASA's launch operations to ensure safety before launches into space. He used flight simulators and worked on space shuttle control systems. After intense training, he was finally chosen to become a mission specialist. A mission specialist works closely with the commander and pilot of a space shuttle. They prepare the activities of the shuttle crew. They also monitor the use of fuel, water, and food and conduct spacewalks. This is when an astronaut exits a ship and moves around in space. They must wear a suit that provides them with oxygen. Astronauts usually go on spacewalks to make repairs and perform maintenance on the space station.

In November 2002, John flew to the International Space Station aboard the *Endeavour* shuttle. The International Space Station is 250 miles above Earth and travels at a speed of 17,500 miles per hour in orbit around the planet. The purpose of the space station is to learn more about how humans can live and work in space. John's mission was to relieve the old crew, send them back to Earth, transfer cargo, and install equipment. He performed three spacewalks and helped maintain temperature controls to ensure the astronauts didn't get too hot or cold.

John is a member of the Chickasaw Nation, which makes him the first native man from a federally recognized tribe to visit space. On his 13-day trip to the International Space Station, he brought the Chickasaw Nation flag, arrowheads, and his own flute. He also brought a braid of sweetgrass and some eagle feathers. Sweetgrass is a long prairie grass that is important to native culture. It is braided together and dried, then lit on fire on one end. The smoke is waved over a person to keep away negative energy. Eagle feathers are also viewed with great respect.

John enjoyed his experience living and working in space. He slept on the ceiling and watched as his books floated in midair. His involvement with NASA brought more attention to Native American participation in science programs. Before John went to space in 2002, NASA celebrated with hundreds of native community leaders and representatives. He was also inducted into the Chickasaw Hall of Fame.

In 2004, John became the commander of an underwater laboratory called Aquarius. The purpose of the lab is to prepare astronauts for future space exploration, since being underwater is similar to being in space. Astronauts train underwater in a pool that is 40 feet deep, 200 feet long, and 100 feet wide, all inside their space suit! He spent 10 days living and working underwater.

John has won many awards, such as the Navy Commendation Medal, the Coast Guard Meritorious Unit Commendation, Sea Service Deployment Ribbons, and the National Defense Service Medal. He is a lifetime member of the Association of Naval Aviation. He met his wife, Margo Aragon, while on a cross-country bicycle trip. They have two children. In 2013, he began working on his doctorate degree in education.

> **"REALIZE THAT NATIVE AMERICANS, OR MEMBERS OF ANY OTHER UNDERREPRESENTED MINORITY, MAKE GREAT SCIENTISTS IF THEY ARE WILLING TO WORK HARD AND STAY FOCUSED ON THEIR DREAM."**

John retired from the Navy and NASA in 2005, and later began speaking to students at schools across the country to teach them about space travel. He works with the Chickasaw Nation to promote interest in science and higher education. He also encourages young people to stay motivated and pursue their goals. He plans to become a teacher and help children fulfill their dreams. His experiences as an astronaut would inspire any child who is lucky enough to have him as their teacher.

THINK IT THROUGH

Why do you think John brought native items like feathers and arrowheads into space with him? What items from your own heritage or family would you want to bring?

EXPLORE MORE!

Learn more about the Chickasaw Nation and discover the values and culture John Herrington grew up with by visiting Chickasaw.net.

Debra
ANNE HAALAND
{ 1960-Present }
LAGUNA PUEBLO

Debra Haaland is the first Native American to become the head of the Department of the Interior. She is also the first woman to lead this government agency. Many Native Americans are glad to see her in this role, as her presence brings more awareness to native issues.

Debra was born in Winslow, Arizona, on December 2, 1960. She is a member of the Laguna Pueblo Tribal Nation. Her father was John David Haaland, a Norwegian American born in New London, Minnesota. He was a US Marine and a recipient of the Silver Star Medal. He served 30 years in the US military and passed away in 2005. Her mother is Mary Toya, a US Navy veteran who worked at the Bureau of Indian Affairs for 25 years. Mary joined the Navy right after high school. She met John when they were both in the Navy. They had five children together. Debra attended 13 different public schools. She spent most summers with her Pueblo grandparents baking bread in a house with no water.

Debra's grandfather left the Pueblo community to work as a diesel train mechanic. He worked for 45 years on the railroads in Winslow, Arizona. He passed down the Pueblo language and traditions to his children and grandchildren. Some of Debra's best memories are of spending time with her grandfather picking worms off cornstalks near her village and eating peaches under a tree. Debra is proud that she came from Pueblo farmers. Her connection to New Mexico is rooted in her Laguna Pueblo heritage. The Laguna Pueblo likely first arrived in the area of New Mexico around the 1200s.

After Debra graduated from Highland High School in Albuquerque, New Mexico, she briefly worked for a bakery before enrolling at the University of New Mexico. She graduated with a bachelor's degree in English in 1994. She was 28.

Debra gave birth to her only daughter, Somáh, shortly after graduation. It was a challenging time. They were poor and had to get food stamps to buy food when money was low. She struggled with alcoholism. They were temporarily homeless and moved around a lot. She started a small salsa business called Pueblo Salsa to make extra money.

Debra went back to the University of New Mexico and earned a degree in federal Indian law in 2006. She started to get more involved with helping improve the Pueblo community. She was a chairwoman of the Laguna Development Corporation Board of Directors and was successful in developing environmentally friendly business policies. In interviews, Debra has said she got into politics because she simply "wanted more Native Americans to vote."

She became a full-time campaign volunteer in 2008, calling people to encourage them to vote for Barack Obama. In 2010, she volunteered for Diane Denish's campaign to become lieutenant governor of New Mexico. Among other responsibilities, the lieutenant governor takes over when the governor is out of state or cannot complete their duties. Two years later, Debra worked for Obama's re-election campaign as the Native American vote director. She visited many native communities across the state of New Mexico encouraging people to vote.

Debra decided to run for lieutenant governor of New Mexico in 2014. She lost the election, but became the chair of the New Mexico Democratic Party from 2015 to 2017. Her duties were leading meetings and serving as the official spokesperson of the organization.

In 2018, Debra decided to run for the US House of Representatives in New Mexico's first congressional district. She won with 59 percent of the vote, becoming one of the first two Native American women elected to Congress. The other native woman elected to Congress was Sharice Davids from the Ho-Chunk Nation. During the swearing in ceremony, Debra wore a traditional Pueblo dress, boots, and necklace.

Debra's decision to run for Congress was born out of her love for New Mexico and the need to help with issues such as teen suicide, women's reproductive rights, climate change, access to childcare, and economic equality. Debra has insisted more people like her need to represent their communities in Congress.

Her ability to overcome alcoholism inspired other native women to break the cycle of addiction. Native American communities have a higher rate of alcohol abuse than any other group in the country. Paulene Abeyta is a member of the Navajo Nation and lost her mother to alcoholism. Paulene said that she wanted to help improve her own community after seeing Debra's rise. Paulene ran for a school board seat and won. Debra was there when Paulene was sworn in.

Debra's daughter, Somáh, is now a poet, performer, writer, and activist. Somáh credits her mother for inspiring her to make the world a better place and to "do the right thing." When Somáh was in high school, she came out to her mother as queer. Debra was supportive and is very proud of her daughter. In 2015, the US Supreme Court upheld **marriage equality**, and Debra was excited that Somáh could marry whomever she wants.

After President Joe Biden was elected, he nominated Debra for the role of Secretary of the Interior. She officially became head of the Department of the Interior on March 15, 2021. This agency has a variety of responsibilities, including overseeing the Bureau of Indian Affairs, the Bureau of Indian Education, and the Bureau of Land Management.

Debra is the first Native American cabinet secretary in American history. She is a strong advocate for native women, the environment, the LGBTQ+ community, **universal health care**, and dismantling the Immigration and Customs Enforcement agency. She also supported the Standing Rock protests, in which native activists tried to stop an oil pipeline from being built through their land.

Debra's achievements show people what they can accomplish when they work hard to make a difference. She faced many challenges, especially as a single mother going to school. Her connection to her culture and the positive influence of her family helps her be strong. Her past experiences also help her understand what many other Americans go through. Many people can find inspiration in her success and be encouraged to make positive changes.

THINK IT THROUGH

Why is it important to have people from different backgrounds and cultures in government?

EXPLORE MORE!

Learn about the Pueblo of Laguna's six villages and its history at LagunaPueblo-NSN.gov.

Glossary

activist: A person who campaigns to bring about political or social change through protesting, speaking, writing, and networking

advocate: To speak or act in favor of

Alcatraz Island: A rocky island in the San Francisco Bay that served as a prison from 1859 to 1963 and is now a tourist attraction

ancestors: The people from whom a person is descended

anthropology: The study of humans and their societies and cultures

archaeologist: Someone who studies remains of human life or society

artifacts: Objects made by human beings

assimilate: To become part of a larger culture

ballerina: A female dancer who must dance with grace in a flowing pattern to tell a story

Black Hills: Mountains located in southwestern South Dakota and northeastern Wyoming that are sacred to the Lakota, Dakota, and Nakota tribes

buckskin: Soft leather made from a buck, or male deer

buffalo: A large North American mammal that has thick dark brown fur and a shaggy mane over the head and neck, with short horns and a large hump above the shoulders, and was the primary food source for Native Americans living on the plains

cavalry: An army on horseback

choreographer: someone who plans the movements of a dance

civil rights movement: A time of struggle during the 1950s and 1960s when Black people in the United States fought to end racial discrimination and have equal rights

colonization: The act of forcefully settling in an area to control resources and overpower the indigenous population

confederacy: A group of people joined for a shared purpose

culture: The customs, arts, social institutions, and achievements of a particular nation, people, or other social group

diagnosis: Identification of a disease based on symptoms

dialects: Particular ways of speaking that are specific to a region or social group

encroachment: The gradual intrusion into someone's land or rights

ethnology: The study of culture or comparing cultures

eulogy: Speech in honor of a person who has died

excavation site: An area where remains are found and studied

flint: A hard form of the mineral quartz

folklore: Traditional stories from a culture or group of people

game: Animals hunted for food

geologist: A scientist who studies the history of the Earth

guerrilla fighters: Armed people who attack through methods like raids and ambushes

heritage: Something that is passed down from previous generations

hostile: Showing dislike or anger

indigenous: The earliest known inhabitants of a place

injustices: Violations of the rights of others

javelin: A slim, metal shaft that can be thrown a long distance by an athlete on an athletic field

latrine: A toilet or outhouse

legacy: What someone leaves behind when they die, such as their accomplishments or the impact they have made

literate: Able to read

marriage equality: A situation in which both same-sex and opposite-sex couples have the right to marry

mascot: A person, animal, or thing used as a symbolic figure to bring good luck

medicine man: A woman or man who may have the power to heal someone who is sick using plants, prayers, and songs

militiamen: Citizens who are not soldiers but act as a military in an emergency

missionary: A person sent on a religious mission to promote their beliefs (often Christianity) in a foreign country

mourning: Feeling or showing great sadness

musicologist: Someone who studies music

National Football League: The major professional football league in the United States, with 31 teams across two conferences

Olympics: A modern version of the ancient Greek Olympic Games now held during the winter and summer seasons

opera: A play in which most words are sung and the music comes from an orchestra

oral tradition: Knowledge and information passed down through generations but not written down

outhouse: A small outdoor shack containing a toilet with no plumbing or running water

paleontologist: A scientist who studies the past through fossil remains

prehistoric: From before written history

prisoners of war: People captured by the enemy during war

purgatory: In religion, a place or state of suffering after death

Quaker: A member of a Christian movement based on simplicity and peacefulness

rations: Portions of food

recruit: To get to join

renowned: Famous and respected

repatriation: The act of returning ceremonial items held by museums to native tribes

replica: A copy or model

reservation: A tract of public land set aside for use by Native Americans

sacred: Holy, deserving of great respect

scout: A person sent to gather information

settlers: People who come to live in a new area

social justice: Fairness in rights and opportunities

sovereignty: Supreme power or freedom

spiritual: Of or relating to sacred matters or concerned with religious values

syllabary: A series of written characters that represent syllables

tomahawk: A light ax used as a hand weapon

trade school: A school that trains students in a specific skill to prepare them for jobs

traditional: Adhering to past practices or usual behavior

treaty: An agreement or arrangement made between two political groups

tumultuous: Full of noise or disorder

understudy: A performer who learns the main performer's role to act as a substitute

universal health care: A system in which everyone has access to free or affordable health care

warriors: People engaged in or experienced in warfare, combat, and conflict

Resources

Museums
National Museum of the American Indian, Washington, DC
AmericanIndian.si.edu

Millicent Rogers Museum, Taos, New Mexico
MillicentRogers.org

Sequoyah Birthplace Museum
SequoyahMuseum.org

Museum of Native American History, Bentonville, Arizona
Monah.us

Eiteljorg Museum, Indianapolis, Indiana
Eiteljorg.org

Websites
Cherokee Nation
Cherokee.org

Shawnee Tribe
Shawnee-NSN.gov

Navajo Nation
Navajo-NSN.gov

The Osage Nation
OsageNation-NSN.gov

Omaha Tribe of Nebraska
OmahaTribe.com

Dakota Wicohan
DakotaWicohan.org

References

Brown, Dee. *Bury My Heart at Wounded Knee: An Indian History of the American West.* New York: Holt, Rinehart and Winston, 1970.

Changing the Face of Medicine. "Dr. Susan LaFlesche Picotte." Last modified June 3, 2015. CFMedicine .NLM.NIH.gov/physicians/biography_253.html.

Deloria, Philip. "Tecumseh's Doomed Quest for a Native Confederacy." *New Yorker,* November 2, 2020.

Georgia Historical Society. "Sequoyah and the Cherokee Syllabary." GeorgiaHistory.com/education-outreach /online-exhibits/featured-historical-figures /sequoyah/talking-leaves.

Geronimo. *Geronimo: The True Story of America's Most Ferocious Warrior.* Edited by S. M. Barrett. New York: Skyhorse Publishing, 2011.

Jenkins, Sally. "Why Are Jim Thorpe's Olympic Records Still Not Recognized?" *Smithsonian Magazine.* July 2012. SmithsonianMag.com/history/why-are -jim-thorpes-olympic-records-still-not-recognized -130986336.

Mankiller, Wilma, and Michael Wallis. *Mankiller: A Chief and Her People.* New York: St. Martin's Press, 1994.

Means, Russell, and Marvin J. Wolf. *Where White Men Fear to Tread: The Autobiography of Russell Means.* New York: Macmillan, 1995.

Preucel, Robert W. "An Archaeology of NAGPRA: Conversations with Suzan Shown Harjo." *Journal of Social Archaeology* 11, no. 2 (June 2011): 130–143.

Shapland, Jenn. "New Mexico Women: Deb Haaland." *Southwest Contemporary,* January 30, 2019. SouthwestContemporary.com/new-mexico-women -deb-haaland.

Short, Candy Franklin. "Tallchief, Marjorie Louise." *The Encyclopedia of Oklahoma History and Culture.* OKHistory.org/publications/enc/entry.php?entry =TA007.

Society for American Archaeology. "New Award Honors Bertha Parker Cody, First US Native American Woman Archaeologist." November 16, 2020. SAA.org /quick-nav/saa-media-room/saa-news/2020/11/16 /bertha-parker-cody-award.

Wilkins, David E. *Red Prophet: The Punishing Intellectualism of Vine Deloria, Jr.* Golden, CO: Fulcrum Publishing, 2018.

Wilson, Linda D. "Herrington, John Bennett." *The Encyclopedia of Oklahoma History and Culture.* OKHistory .org/publications/enc/entry.php?entry=HE024.

Women & the American Story. "Life Story: Zitkala-Sa, aka Gertrude Simmons Bonnin (1876–1938)." WAMS.NYHistory.org/modernizing-america /xenophobia-and-racism/zitkala-sa.

Author Acknowledgments

Thank you to my editor, Mary Colgan, for her kind support in helping me write this book. I appreciate Ashley Popp for reaching out to me and taking a chance. Thank you to my wife, Ramona Cliff, who has pushed me to keep writing and expressing myself. Thank you to my children for their patience and understanding when dad had to write. A big thank-you to my mom, Madelyn Beason, who always encouraged me to read and learn. Thank you to my brother, Chris Ross, for his words of support. Thank you to Aunt Ann, Grandma, Papa, Derek, Morin, Uncle Mike, Uncle Roger, Danielle, Kyler, and Vanessa—all my family, whose love kept me going.

About the Author

Jimmy Lee Beason II is a member of the Osage Nation of Oklahoma. He is from the Eagle Clan. He has a bachelor's degree in Indigenous and American Indian Studies from Haskell Indian Nations University. He earned his master's degree in social work from the University of Kansas. He writes nonfiction, fiction, poetry, and essays about contemporary native issues. He lives in Lawrence, Kansas, with his wife, Ramona Cliff, and three children, Ayo, Mavcyka, and Washoshe. Beason is a professor at Haskell Indian Nations University in the Indigenous and American Indian Studies Department.

Illustrator Acknowledgments

Thank you to my beautiful family and encouraging group of friends for the support, humor, and light over this past year and beyond.

About the Illustrator

 **Amanda Lenz** is an illustrator and designer residing in Boulder, Colorado. The love of the outdoors, people, places, and adventure shines through her illustrative work. Ten years in a solo design and illustration practice (LenzIllustration.com) has borne a variety of rich visual work. A fine art and figure drawing practice paired with a design and digital sensibility has created her rich, colorful, and crafted illustration style. Amanda loves telling visual stories of inspiring people and the places and ideas they have shaped. She spends her spare time sketching, gardening, and hiking with her partner and two adorable, slightly rotten dogs.

Printed in the USA
CPSIA information can be obtained
at www.ICGtesting.com
CBHW080516290124
R14841000001B/R148410PG3539CBX00004B/1